The Ultimate Guide to Pothos Plants

The Ultimate Guide to Pothos Plants

Epipremnum, Philodendron & Scindapsus Varieties, Care & Propagation

Marianne D. Baesa

ISBN: 9798562797452

Cover design by Marianne D. Baesa

Seek growth, not perfection.

TABLE OF CONTENTS

INTRODUCTION

The Ultimate Guide to Pothos Plants is a reference and instructional guide for house plant enthusiasts and collectors to help them correctly identify different pothos plant varieties, and how to successfully care for and propagate them.

This book describes around fifty different varieties, cultivars, and forms of pothos under the Epipremnum, Scindapsus and Philodendron plant varieties.

The decision on which varieties to include in this guidebook is based on plants scientifically classified as pothos, and plants considered as pothos by the horticultural field, plant growers and sellers, and by the house plant community, accounting their classification history and naming trends in recent the years.

This means that there are varieties, cultivars, and forms included in here that might be commonly referred to as pothos but are not currently scientifically named as such. Vice versa, there are varieties, cultivars, and forms also scientifically or historically recognized as pothos, such as varieties under the Scindapsus species, but are not included in varieties of pothos listed in this book.

Therefore, **Epipremnum** pothos mentioned here are limited to popular varieties, cultivars, and forms of plants classified as Epipremnum Aureum and Epipremnum Pinnatum.

Philodendron pothos-like plants identified here are limited to popular varieties, cultivars, and forms classified under Philodendron Hederaceum, Philodendron Scandens, or Philodendron Cordatum.

Scindapsus pothos-like plants identified here are limited to popular varieties, cultivars, and forms classified under Scindapsus Pictus, Scindapsus Lucens, and Scindapsus Treubii.

As the different varieties of pothos are described, terms such as variety, cultivar, form, sport, and/or mutation are often used, and used as accurately as possible in describing each plant.

However, these terms are largely loosely defined, and often used interchangeably in the horticultural world and in the house plant community, and therefore their usage here might also appear inconsistent.

As this guide is geared towards beginners, instructions on how to care for pothos plants are focused on the basics of water, light, and soil. Tips on how to successfully propagate pothos are focused on the fundamentals of water propagation and propagating in various inert mediums.

Additionally, two bonus chapters from the author's next book, **House Plants Back to Basics**, covers “How to Flush House Plants” and “Understanding Yellowing Leaves in House Plants” are found at the end.

Information shared in this book is based on research cited and listed in the reference section, and from the author's personal experience caring for nearly fifty varieties of pothos in her plant collection.

While *The Ultimate Guide to Pothos Plants* is targeted towards new plant parents and pothos collectors, any plant enthusiasts or horticulture student can also benefit from having this book as a quick but informative reference guide on learning the different varieties of pothos plants, as well as instructions on their proper care and successful propagation.

POTHOS PLANT VARIETIES

Pothos plants are arguably the most popular house plant. Even for people who are not plant collectors, they will likely have had a pothos plant in their spaces at one point.

Most well-known varieties of pothos are quite common and affordable, can grow in under any type of light, including under a fluorescent light, easy to care for and propagate, and looks good in any part of interior decor, from any living to working spaces.

However, there are also "rare" or uncommon pothos varieties that can easily rival currently trending "rare" plants in the plant community, but without the same price tag.

Pothos plants originated from Moorea in French Polynesia, but several varieties are also native to many Pacific Islands and Southeast Asian countries. Many cultivars are also introduced by growers in the United States, such as Costa Farms and Gabriella Plants.

While the exact effectiveness is debated, pothos are well-known indoor air purifying plants, and can help purify air of chemicals, including formaldehyde, trichloroethene, toluene, xylene, and benzene (Ianotti).

Golden pothos is the most well-known variety of pothos, as it is the most commonly available house plant pretty much anywhere in the world; but new plant parents are often surprised to learn there are multiple varieties of pothos plants.

Exact number of pothos plant varieties is undetermined, as pothos plants have changed classification multiple times, and have multiple common names used within the horticultural field and the house plant community. Some varieties are possibly currently unknown, and new cultivars are being created by growers in recent years.

The widely accepted classification of pothos is Epipremnum Aureum, and its varieties are what is primarily considered as pothos plants. However, there are Scindapsus and Philodendron varieties, cultivars, and forms that are also often referred to or considered as pothos by the house plant community.

For example, some vining Philodendron plants are often mistaken for pothos and vice versa, likely because they both belong to the arum family or aroids. Their most common varieties can also look very similar to the untrained eye and have very similar care and growth pattern with Epipremnum pothos plants.

In the early 1900s, pothos were first classified as Scindapsus Aurea, which likely correlates to Scindapsus varieties that the house plant community still considers as pothos or are commonly sold as satin pothos or silver pothos. Many Scindapsus varieties are also still listed scientifically as pothos.

Moreover, as the plant community rapidly grows, especially with the help of social media and e-commerce in recent years, multiple common names are given to different or similar varieties of pothos for identification and commercialization purposes, which are often interchangeable and redundant.

The Ultimate Guide to Pothos Plants helps plant enthusiasts identify around fifty different varieties, cultivars and forms of pothos classified under Epipremnum, Philodendron, and Scindapsus species.

The official name of each variety used here is their most updated name officially recorded and listed in scientific journals, and in equally reliable horticultural sources, as well as their commonly accepted names within the house plant community.

EPIPREMNUM POTHOS

The plant species with the most pothos varieties, cultivars, and forms is the Epipremnum. Easily recognized pothos plants are officially classified as Epipremnum Aureum, but some Epipremnum Pinnatum varieties are considered as pothos as well.

For most Epipremnum pothos, the basic shape of their leaves is a slightly narrow heart-shaped leaf. As a new leaf grows, its petiole separates from the vine, and has no free stipules on the new growth, so their petioles are grooved (North Carolina State Extension).

In the wild, they are often understory plants and act as ground cover but are also seen climbing up trees. When they do, some varieties can grow huge leaves and form fenestrations like the Monstera Deliciosa.

However, as indoor plants, most pothos varieties can be trained to climb up by providing them a moss pole or a trellis; otherwise, pothos vines will naturally trail down.

Most pothos leaves can remain green in low light and are generally low feeders, which makes them ideal house plants. While pothos are easy to care for and propagate, pothos plants are shy-flowering plants both in the wild and in cultivation due to their lack of a gene, called Gibberellin, which is responsible for flowering of plants. The last observed flowers of Epipremnum Aureum were in a lab in 1962 (Hung et al.).

Pothos plants can live up to 10 years (Douglass) and can grow up to 30 feet long (Ianotti). Since they are so easy to propagate and are fast growers, they are considered invasive when planted outdoors, especially where they are not native. They are a perennial vining plant, so they make great hanging indoor plants, and give off that indoor jungle feel in any space.

Other common names of the pothos plant include but not limited to: Devil's Ivy, Hunter's Robe, Golden Vine, Taro Vine, and Money Plant.

Epipremnum Aureum varieties are the most common and easily accessible pothos plants. They go by multiple common names, and some can look remarkably similar, but have distinct enough differences to be considered their own forms.

Epipremnum Pinnatum varieties are considered more uncommon outside of their place of origin, and sometimes sold as rare plants. They can look widely different from most Epipremnum Aureum pothos varieties and are often mistaken for Monstera and Rhaphidophora plants.

EPIPREMNUM POTHOS

Jade

Golden

Hawaiian Golden

Jessenia

Neon

Var. Neon

Marble Queen

Snow Queen

N'Joy

Glacier

Pearls &
Jade

Manjula

Global Green

Emerald

Manjula
Sport

Rev. Manjula

JADE

Jade pothos (also known as Green Queen pothos or Tropic Green pothos) is the most basic variety of Epipremnum Aureum pothos. Its heart shaped leaves have no variegation and are medium to dark green in color.

GOLDEN

Golden pothos are medium green to dark green leaf pothos often with white and golden-yellow variegation, but many of its individual leaves can also be purely green without any variegation. The Golden pothos is the most commonly sold pothos plant and the variety of pothos that most people have.

HAWAIIAN GOLDEN

Hawaiian Golden pothos leaves have dense but fragmented yellow variegation over dark green, and its stems are usually more yellow than green. When mature, it is also known for having larger leaves compared to Golden pothos.

JESSENIA

Another sport of the Golden pothos, Jessenia pothos is a cultivar from Costa Farms, a well-known grower and wholesaler of house plants in the United States. It has a mix of both emerald green and chartreuse variegation, with a marbling and mosaic like pattern on its leaves.

Jessenia Pothos
© IG: @mytinygreenuniverse

NEON

Neon pothos have bright lime or neon green leaves as opposed to the medium to dark green of the Jade pothos. The younger leaves tend to start out as more neon yellow, and then turn into neon green as it matures.

Neon Pothos
© Marianne Baesa

VARIEGATED NEON

Variegated Neon pothos is a mutated form of the *Neon* pothos with dark green, white and/or golden-yellow variegation on its leaves. The variegation can appear in splashes, sections or marbling on the leaves.

Variegated Neon Pothos
© Marianne Baesa

MARBLE QUEEN

Marble Queen pothos has the same shape of leaf and variegation pattern as the Golden pothos. However, the Marble Queen pothos's variegation is a mix of green, light green, and white in different watercolor-like marbling, often referred to as albo variegation in the plant community.

The variegation also occurs at a higher rate and exists in almost every leaf, but often in irregular patterns, and can produce "half-moon" leaves, wherein half of the leaf is completely green and the other half is variegated.

Marble Queen Pothos
© Marianne Baesa

SNOW QUEEN

Snow Queen pothos is a sport of the Marble Queen pothos, and this form mainly has white leaves with fine watercolor-like splashes or speckles of green. This is consistent throughout most if not all the leaves of a Snow Queen pothos. Stems are also largely white with little to no green.

Snow Queen Pothos
© Marianne Baesa

PEARLS AND JADE

Pearls and Jade pothos is a mutated form of the Marble Queen pothos. It has irregularly shaped but solid green variegation that is often found in the middle of the leaf and is surrounded by white variegation with splashes of green, similar to the Snow Queen pothos' variegation.

Pearls & Jade Pothos
© Marianne Baesa

GLACIER

Glacier pothos is nearly identical to Pearls and Jade pothos, but without the green speckles or splashes on the white parts of its leaves. It also has a silver gray molting that often gradients between the solid green and solid white variegation of the leaves.

N'JOY

N'Joy pothos is often mistaken for the Glacier pothos, but the key difference between the two is the N'Joy pothos does not have silver-grey molting found on the Glacier pothos. It only has white and green solid variegation, with the green color mostly found on the inside.

EMERALD

Emerald pothos is one of the newest cultivars of pothos, and it looks like an N'Joy or Glacier pothos that has lost its white variegation but has kept the variegation pattern in different shades of green. The darker shade of green is often found inside and the lighter shade on the outside.

Emerald Pothos
© Marianne Baesa

GLOBAL GREEN

Global Green pothos is also one of the latest pothos cultivar. It is a Japanese cultivar with only 500 plants released initially in the U.S. in 2020 (Monstera Mike), but it is also reported as a patented cultivar from Costa Farms.

It looks remarkably similar to the Emerald pothos, but while the Emerald pothos has the lighter green or chartreuse variegation on the edge of the leaf, the Global Green pothos has the lighter variegation inside of the leaf.

Global Green Pothos
© IG: @the.plantnurse & @pothosloco

MANJULA

Manjula pothos is a cultivar from the University of Florida that has a similar coloring as the Marble Queen pothos, and sometimes the Pearls and Jade pothos as well, but with a different pattern of variegation.

What definitively distinguishes the Manjula pothos is it has wider spade-like shaped leaves, which are often slightly curled or wavy, and its variegation pattern often follows the contours of the leaves.

A possible sport of the Manjula pothos is the Harlequin pothos, which is a Manjula pothos with higher amounts of solid white variegation with no green speckles on the white parts.

Manjula Pothos
© Marianne Baesa

MANJULA SPORT SP

This is a sport of the Manjula pothos, which can look very similar to the Global Green pothos at first glance, but its differentiating characteristic is it has the same spade-like shape of the Manjula pothos leaves.

More importantly, it retains the same variegation pattern of the Manjula pothos with at least two shades of green and no white variegation. This sport is currently officially unidentified but is given a common name of *Marianne* pothos by the author, who currently owns this sport of Manjula pothos.

Marianne Pothos
© Marianne Baesa

REVERTED MANJULA SP

Another unidentified or yet to be named sport of Manjula pothos is a Manjula pothos that appears to have completely reverted to green. Unlike the previous Manjula Sport s.p. pothos, this does not have anyvariegation pattern, only fully green leaves.

What contrasts this reverted Manjula s.p. pothos from the Jade pothos is still it retains more of the round spade-like wavy shape of the leaves of the Manjula pothos.

Reverted Manjula Pothos
© Marianne Baesa

The following are documented pothos varieties in horticultural journals and reputable botanical websites. Aside from statements claiming that they do exist or existed at the time of their documentation, particularly in the journal article, "A Review of Epipremnum (Araceae) in Cultivation," by Peter Boyce, as of writing very little information or no recent images can be found on them.

MAYAN GOLD

Mayan Gold pothos is possibly another sport of the Golden pothos with golden yellow leaves that is richer in color (Boyce).

JOHANNA QUEEN

Johanna Queen pothos is registered with Vaste Keurings Commissie in 1993 as a variety of pothos that has "dark green leaves with irregular pale marbling." It does not seem to be currently cultivated or available commercially (Boyce).

GREEN GENIE

Green Genie pothos is a cultivar that is a smaller plant with smaller leaves than the Marble Queen pothos. It has a dark green color with a lighter green color on the underside of its leaves (Henny et al.). Its leaves are also waxy and thicker in comparison to the Marble Queen pothos (Florida Foundation Seed Producers, Inc.).

EPIPREMNUM WILCOXII

The Epipremnum Wilcoxii shares similar and almost indistinguishable characteristics with Epipremnum Aureum Hawaiian Golden. It has dense yellow variegation that is very fragmented, thus giving it a golden yellow and green marbling variegation (Boyce).

EPIPREMNUM PINNATUM

CEBU BLUE

Cebu Blue pothos is native to the Philippines in Southeast Asia, and named after the city of its origin, Cebu, which is in the Visayas region in the Philippines.

Its leaves are green with a distinct silvery bluish tone. It has the same narrow heart shaped leaves as other pothos, but the leaves are much more elongated, and has a more textured surface.

Cebu Blue Pothos
© Marianne Baesa

DRAGON TAIL

Epipremnum Pinnatum, commonly called Tibatib or Dragon Tail pothos, is often mistaken for the Cebu Blue pothos in its juvenile form, or the Monstera Deliciosa when its mature leaves are fenestrated (Long). It is found originally in the Luzon region in the Philippines.

The key difference between the two is its leaves are green and do not have the silver-blue coloring of the Cebu Blue pothos. While most pothos are considered toxic when ingested, Tibatib is considered as a medicinal plant (Stuart Change).

Epipremnum Pinnatum
© peaceloveandhappiness.club

EPIPREMNUM PINNATUM VARIEGATA

Epipremnum Pinnatum also has a variegated form that is gaining popularity within the house plant community, the Epipremnum Pinnatum Variegata, which has a similar variegation to the Monstera Deliciosa Albo Variegata.

SKELETON KEY

Skeleton Key pothos is an aroid that is often mistaken as a Dragon Tail pothos or Jade pothos in its juvenile form. As the leaves mature, the bottom half of the leaves will remain wide, while the top half narrows into strip, giving the leaf a shape similar to a key (House Plant Hobbyist).

Skeleton Key Pothos
© Marianne Baesa & IG: @earthplants.id

SHANGRILA

Shangri-La pothos look like regular pothos when their leaves are unfurled; but as the leaves mature, they curl and form the shape of a cone. Compared to most pothos, they are slow growers.

It also goes by the names Godzilla, Javelin, Witch's Hat and Sleeping pothos (Happy Houseplants).

Shangrila Pothos
© IG: @mamhike

SHANGRI-OOHLALA

Shangri Ooh Lala pothos is a variegated form of the Shangri-La or Sleeping pothos. It has golden yellow variegation like the Golden pothos but is a much slower grower (New Life Tropicals).

Shangri Oohlala Pothos
© Marianne Baesa

PHILODENDRON POTHOS

Native to Mexico, Latin America, and West Indies, some Philodendron plants that vine or climb are often mistaken for or are often compared to pothos in the house plant community.

These are often of the Philodendron Hederaceum variety, and these vining philodendrons have wider and rounder heart shaped leaves compared to Epipremnum Aureum pothos.

When growing a new leaf, the growth often tends to point or grow upward. They also often grow aerial roots faster than Epipremnum and Scindapsus pothos plants.

Younger leaves and stems also start out as peach or pink in color, and their petiole remains fully round while the petiole of Epipremnum pothos are indented or grooved after it separates from the vine.

PHILODENDRON POTHOS

Heartleaf

Lime

Var. Lime

Brasil

Rio

Silver Stripe

Cream Splash

Gabby

Brandtianum

Heartleaf Variegata

Mican

HEARTLEAF

Heartleaf Philodendron (aka philodendron scandens, philodendron cordatum, philodendron oxycardium, philodendron hederaceum) is the philodendron counterpart of the Jade pothos.

All its leaves are green when they mature and have no variegation in them. The key difference between Jade pothos and Heartleaf Philodendron is in the shape of their leaves and petioles. The Heartleaf Philodendron has a rounder, wider leaf than Jade pothos.

Heartleaf Philodendron
© Marianne Baesa

LIME

Philodendron *Lime* (a.k.a. lemon, goldilocks, neon) shares the same bright chartreuse or light yellow-green color of the Neon pothos, but with the leaf shape and growth pattern of a Heartleaf Philodendron.

Philodendron Lime
© Marianne Baesa

VARIEGATED LIME

Variegated Lime Philodendron is a Philodendron Lime that produces leaves with dark green, light green, and golden yellow variegation. This sport or form of the lime is not as widely recognized as the variegated neon pothos, as it is not yet determined as stable, the variegation could just be a result of reverting, and can potentially end up looking similar to a Philodendron Brasil.

Philodendron Lime Variegata
© Marianne Baesa

BRASIL

Philodendron Brasil is green with lemon lime variegation that is often found in the middle. However, its leaves can also sometimes be half green and half lime, or fully lime, so the pattern of the variegation is not uniformed.

RIO SPORT

A sport of the Philodendron Brasil originally cultivated by Gabriella Plants in Florida, USA, Philodendron Rio Sport has the variegation of silver, cream and dark green, with silver as its most center color.

Philodendron Rio Sport
© Marianne Baesa

SILVER STRIPE

Philodendron Silver Stripe is another sport of the Philodendron Brasil similar to the Philodendron Rio Sport, and as the name suggests, has a silver stripe variegation in the middle, as well as cream and lime.

Philodendron Silver Stripe
© Marianne Baesa

CREAM SPLASH

Philodendron Cream Splash is another sport of the Philodendron Brasil that is very similar to the Philodendron Silver Stripe and is also a mutation from Philodendron Brasil. It has the variegation of light green, dark green and cream.

This sport is often confused with either the Philodendron Silver Stripe or Philodendron Gabby due to their close similarities.

Philodendron Cream Splash
© Marianne Baesa

GABBY SPORT

Philodendron Gabby Sport is another cultivar from Gabriella Plants and was referred to as Philodendron Cream Splash when it was first posted and popularized on Pinterest by a plant enthusiast.

However, what differentiates the Philodendron Gabby Sport is its variegation is often unstable and can vary from leaf to leaf. It also can produce leaves that are completely cream in color.

BRANDTIANUM

Philodendron Brandtianum has the same leaf shape as the Heartleaf Philodendron, but has an olive green coloration with grey mottling that is similarly found in many Scindapsus Pictus varieties.

Philodendron Brandtianum
© Marianne Baesa

HEDERACEUM VARIEGATA

Philodendron Hederaceum Variegata have marbled streaks of cream and grey-green variegation, similar to the Marble Queen pothos (Glasshouse Works).

Philodendron Hederaceum Variegata
© Marianne Baesa

VELVET LEAF

Velvet Leaf Philodendron or Philodendron Mican looks like the Heartleaf Philodendron, but the leaves are darker green, sometimes even burgundy in color, and the leaves have a velvety texture to them.

Other forms of the Velvet Leaf Philodendron include: the Micans Ekwador, which has a slightly narrower and longer leaf; and the Philodendron Hederaceum var. Kirkbridei, which is differentiated by its reddish brown and ribbed stems (Aroid.org).

Philodendron Mican
© Marianne Baesa

SCINDAPSUS POTHOS

Native to Southeast Asia, this plant can be grown as a lovely vining houseplant, or alternatively staked to a moss pole to encourage its natural shingling growth pattern. If the moss pole is kept moist and aerial roots attach to the pole, leaves will flatten tightly against the surface and climb vertically, allowing it to shingle.

Before it was classified as Epipremnum Aureum, pothos were classified as Scindapsus, and many Scindapsus varieties are still synonymously classified as pothos. Pictus is the Latin word for painted, which aptly describes the variegation in most Scindapsus Pictus varieties.

There are many other varieties, forms, and cultivars under the Scindapsus genus, about 35 accepted species identified (Boyce and Bogner) and about 69 varieties currently listed in The Plant List online database (The Plant List). Many of these varieties are synonymously referred to as pothos.

Often, varieties of Scindapsus Pictus are sold as silver philodendron, satin pothos, silver pothos, silver satin pothos, or silver splash pothos in nurseries and big box stores as their common name.

For the scope of this group of pothos-like Scindapsus plants listed here, they are limited to the well-known varieties, cultivars, and forms of Scindapsus Pictus, Scindapsus Lucens, and Scindapsus Treubii.

SCINDAPSUS POTHOS

argyraeus

silvery ann

exotica

silver splash

silver lady

jade satin

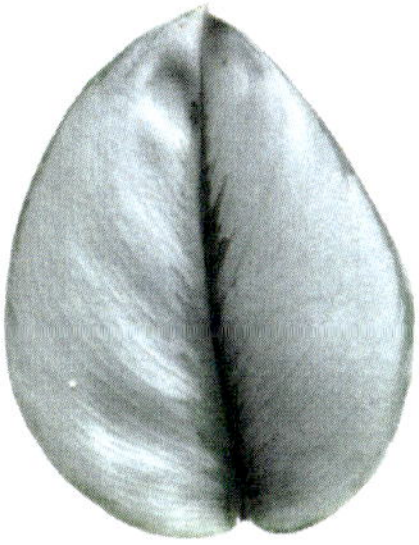
treubii moonlight

lucens

silver hero

treubii dark form

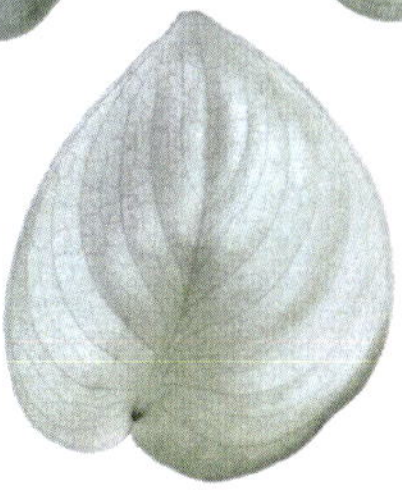
platinum

*variety is Scindapsus Pictus unless otherwise noted

ARGYRAEUS

Scindapsus Pictus Argyraeus' leaves are a bit thicker than the leaves of Philodendron and Epipremnum pothos plants. Their leaves are slightly narrower than heart leaf philodendron but rounder than the Golden pothos.

Its distinctive feature is the small splashes of silver on its matte dark green leaves, and the underside of the leaves are a lighter shade of green. The silver variegation shimmers like glitter when light hits them.

SILVERY ANN

Scindapsus Pictus Silvery Ann often has the same smaller size and shape of leaves as the Scindapsus Pictus Argyraeus, but has a more uneven silver variegation. Often the leaves have more silver than green in them like the Scindapsus Pictus Exotica, but with less consistent variegation pattern. The Silver variegation often starts at the tip of the leaves.

SILVER SPLASH

Scindapsus Pictus Silver Splash has larger leaves compared to Scindapsus Pictus Argyraeus or Silvery Ann, and its silver variegation overlaps with the green, giving it an almost pixelated or mosaic-like appearance.

Scindapsus Silver Splash
© Marianne Baesa

EXOTICA

Scindapsus Pictus Exotica is a Scindapsus variety with plenty of silver variegation that covers most of the leaves except in the middle, which often is the only part of the leaf that is green.

SILVER LADY

Scindapsus Pictus Silver Lady looks similar to the Scindapsus Pictus Exotica, but has more defined edges in its variegation along the midrib and edges of the leaves, as well as where leaf veins are normally found.

Scindapsus Silver Lady
© Marianne Baesa

JADE SATIN

Scindapsus Pictus Jade Satin is a non-variegated Scindapsus Pictus with large dark green leathery leaves. Unlike the Golden pothos or the Heartleaf Philodendron however, Scindapsus Pictus Jade Satin are currently considered more uncommon and sometimes sold for a higher price than the more common variegated Scindapsus Pictus plants.

Scindapsus Jade Satin
© Marianne Baesa

TREUBII MOONLIGHT

Scindapsus Treubii Moonlight is a Scindapsus plant that has a silver sheen and satin-like finish on its light green leaves. It has larger leaves compared to the Scindapsus Pictus Argyraeus. It's also given a common name of Sterling Silver by Costa Farms as part of its 2021 Livetrends Collection.

TREUBII DARK FORM

Scindapsus Treubii Dark Form shares the same characteristics as the Scindapsus Treubii Moonlight, but instead has dark green to near black leaves, which can be similar to the color of the leaves of Zamioculcas Zamiifolia Raven plant or Monstera Standleyana plant.

S. Treubii Dark Form
© Marianne Baesa

SILVER HERO

The Scindapsus Silver Hero is similar to the Jade Satin but with a much lighter almost minty sage green coloring often only seen on the underside of most Scindapsus pictus plants, and has an all over but quite muted, silvery sheen on top of the leaf without any fragmentation seen in many other scindapsus plants with silver variegation.

Scindapsus Silver Hero
© Marianne Baesa

SILVER PLATINUM

The Scindapsus Pictus Silver Platinum was first seen in a private garden in Singapore and introduced by Amos Tan in March 2012. As the name suggests, the leaves are fully metallic with silver-grey green tones that shimmers when hit by light at certain angles (International Aroid Society, Inc.).

The Scindapsus Silver Platinum is also often described as a shinier version of the Scindapsus Silver Hero.

Scindapsus Platinum
© IG: 1000tropicalaroid

SCINDAPSUS LUCENS

Scindapsus Lucens is a "cousin" of the Scindapsus Pictus. In its juvenile form it has greyish to light green leaves (Boyce and Bogner). It also has a defined vein structure that gives it texture similar to Epipremnum Pinnatum Cebu Blue pothos and Monstera Siltepecana. It is often confused with a very similar looking plant, the anadendrum affine.

Scindapsus Lucens
© much.greens

POTHOS PLANT CARE

Pothos can be one of the easiest houseplants to care for - they thrive under most light settings and are not picky with the type of water or soil used on them. They are also low feeders, so they do not require frequent fertilizing, and they do not require high levels of humidity.

However, because they have the reputation as easy-care plants, and plant parents assume they can thrive in any condition, and then are shocked when pothos die under their care. As with any houseplant, learning the language of pothos does take time. The good news is pothos are very resilient plants, and for the most part, can tolerate the growing pains of any new plant parent.

To successfully take care of pothos plants no matter the variety, there are three basic things plant parents must understand and master: light, water, and soil.

LIGHT

Most pothos can thrive under any amount and type of light, from low light to bright indirect light. However, what low light, moderate light, or indirect bright light mean can differ depending on the location and environment.

Luckily for most pothos, as long as they are in a place that gets a decent amount of light, natural or artificial, they can survive in that space.

Nevertheless, low light does not mean no light, even for pothos. If placing pothos in a windowless room or a dark corner, it is best to put it near or under a light source for about eight to twelve hours a day. While under a grow light is preferable, it is not a must, as pothos can grow into a healthy beautiful plant, even under a fluorescent light.

If a pothos plant is hanging from the ceiling or on the wall, or is placed on top of a shelf, light still needs to also reach the top of the pothos, not just its trails. Lack of light on top will cause the pothos to go "bald".

Since pothos do not like overwatering, lack of light will also make the pothos retain water longer, especially if it is in a plastic planter, which can easily lead to root rot. With variegated pothos, the tricky thing is that they need a much higher amount of light to maintain or increase their variegation, but too much light will also burn the leaves, especially the white parts of the leaves.

Moreover, because white variegated leaves lack chlorophyll, they cannot photosynthesize. As a result, they are likely to yellow or brown sooner, and their life cycle is shorter compared to pothos with mostly green leaves no matter the amount of light we give them, and that is something beyond our control. When they continue to receive a very minimal amount of light, variegated pothos plants will start to produce less variegated leaves, and eventually revert back to green.

Therefore, it is best to give variegated pothos moderate to indirect bright light to maintain or encourage more variegation from their leaves. At the same time, to lessen the leaf burns, regularly rotate the pothos plant. If they are placed by a south facing or west facing window, pull them back a foot or two away from those windows, especially during the summer in the northern hemisphere.

Most pothos do well under bright indirect light, but direct light or full sun will most likely result in leaf burn, even for non-variegated pothos.

WATER

Overwatering is the number one killer of pothos.

Pothos can withstand underwatering, and many varieties can bounce back from a short drought, but it does not bounce back easily from overwatering. Just a single incident of overwatering can easily lead to root rot, which can be very difficult to recover from, even for pothos.

In the northern hemisphere, the watering schedule of pothos averages between seven and ten days during the summer, and between 12 and 16 days during the winter.

However, this is not a set standard and having a weekly schedule for watering pothos can be more detrimental than helpful, as it can easily lead to overwatering and killing pothos plants. The best way to know if the pothos needs watering is not by simply counting the days in between watering, but by checking the moisture level of its soil.

The golden rule for watering pothos is to wait for the soil to completely dry before watering. To do that, stick a finger in the soil to check if the soil is dry or not. If little to no soil is attached to the finger when pulled out, then the soil is dry.

However, depending on how big or deep the pot is, only the top two inches or three of the soil can be accurately checked for moisture level using the finger method.

Additional ways to check for moisture level in soil is to check the drainage holes for signs of lingering moisture. This usually is indicated with presence of condensation on the drainage holes or darker soil color.

If moisture around or near the drainage holes are detected, or the soil that is visible through the drainage holes looks darker than the topsoil, then wait a couple more days before watering.

If the pothos is potted in a terracotta pot, check the moisture level by inspecting the pot. Terra cotta pots can absorb and wick moisture, so when the soil is still moist, the terra cotta pot also feels moist and has a darker color compared to when soil is dry.

Another way to tell if the soil is completely dry is when the edge of the top soil starts to separate away from the pot, especially if it is in a plastic pot.

If still unsure if the soil is completely dry, then it is best to wait a couple more days or so before watering. As mentioned earlier, pothos can withstand underwatering, but are susceptible to root rot when overwatered, even just once or twice.

For the most accurate way to tell if soil is dry, use a moisture meter, and water the plant only when the meter reads dry. However, for a number of pothos varieties, moisture level of soil is not enough to indicate if they need watering or not. The leaves also provide additional, and sometimes more accurate, indicators if they are ready for watering, including: softer leaves, yellowing leaves, wrinkled leaves, curling leaves, and overall dull looking foliage.

Most Scindapsus pothos’ leaves curl under to show they already need to be watered. Epipremnum pothos, like the Cebu Blue pothos, produce yellow leaves when not watered on time. Philodendron pothos' entire foliage becomes "flat" and lack "volume", and the leaves start to look wrinkly when their soil has been dry for quite some time.

When it is time to water pothos plants, it is not only how often they are watered, but also how much water they are given. The choice method of watering is something to also consider. Based on anecdotal experience, top watering can easily lead to either underwatering or oversaturating.

When pothos is given more water than it needs, that leads to oversaturated soil. If the water is not properly and completely drained out, the excess water will suffocate the roots and lead to root rot.

Conversely, when pothos is not given enough water, water does not actually reach the root ball, even though it might appear the soil is completely wet. In reality, the water has likely only reached the top inch or two of the soil before the rest had run off to sides and then drained out.

If the preferred method of watering plants is top watering, then important to ensure that enough water is given to the plant, excess water is drained out completely, and to also regularly aerate soil before or after watering.

For most pothos, bottom watering is recommended. This method ensures they are getting just enough water they need. It does take some time to bottom water, but it allows pothos to absorb just the right amount of water it needs. Bottom watering also prevents soil erosion or spillage, soil compacting, and helps with reducing water waste.

To bottom water, place pothos in a tray or container wider than the pot of the pothos, fill the tray up with water to about an inch high or so, depending on width of tray and size of the pothos' pot, as long as the water level is not higher than the height of the pot.

Leave the pothos plant on the tray, and it will take in water via capillary action. When the topsoil of pothos is moist, then it has absorbed all the water it needs. For smaller plants, this can take only a couple of minutes, for pothos in larger pots, it can take a couple of hours. As long as the pothos is not left sitting in water for more than 24 hours, the pothos will be fine.

A concern about bottom watering is mineral and hard water build up in soil. However, pothos are generally not picky with the type of water it takes in, and using tap water to bottom water pothos is more than fine, and like with any house plants, occasionally flushing the pothos will remove mineral build up and excess nutrients in the soil.

After watering pothos, thoroughly drain excess water and give them more light than usual for a few hours. For example, place newly watered pothos plants next to a sunny window or bright light source. This will help dry out excess moisture faster, and therefore prevent root rot or growth of mold and fungus in the soil.

SOIL

Pothos are loved for its vines and the indoor jungle vibe they give to any space, so when there is something wrong with the pothos, plant parents often tend to try to fix what is going on above the soil instead of understanding what is going on underneath the soil.

What most new plant parents are not aware of is the roots dictate what quality of leaves we will get, and how much growth we can expect from our pothos. To get lush leaves and long trailing vines, then take care of the pothos' roots first.

Pothos are generally not picky with their soil, and the soil they come in with when bought from a big box store or nursery is usually fine. As long as they are not yet extremely root bound, which means there are more roots visible than soil when lifted out of the pot, or they do not show any signs of pest presence in the soil, they do not need any immediate repotting.

In fact, they can stay in the soil they came in for as long as they continue to grow and do not show any signs of poor health.

Regularly aerate the soil to allow oxygen to get into the soil for the root to access. Use chopsticks or any blunt slim stick and carefully poke the soil as deep as possible without damaging the roots.

But if and when repotting is needed, use a well-draining potting soil mix. This allows the roots to have access to free oxygen (and not only oxygen in the water) it needs to metabolize and absorb nutrients and minerals.

A well-draining soil for pothos can be any indoor potting mix, do not worry too much about the brand of soil or if it is organic. If typically a heavy waterer, then adding extra perlite or vermiculite to the indoor potting mix will help with soil aeration and drainage. The recommended ratio of perlite to soil is 1:2 or even 1:1.

If and when repotting pothos, a pot with drainage holes is a must. Any type of pot with drainage is fine, but using terra cotta pots are best to use. This avoids locking in any extra moisture that can enable bacterial growth or oxygen deprivation to the roots, which are the leading causes of root rot.

Properly anchor pothos when repotting, which means covering all the roots at the base to ensure the plant does not get easily uprooted, especially when it is already vining.

However, do not overpack the soil as it can also suffocate the roots. Pothos, like most houseplants, need access to oxygen found in between soil particles, not just the oxygen they break down from water.

But how to know when to repot?

Pothos can remain in the same pot and soil for years if they keep growing and look healthy. Repotting should not be a frequent occurrence with pothos, which is why they make great hanging plants.

Pothos prefer to be a little bit rootbound, but if their roots are coming out of its drainage holes, and when lifted off the pot and more roots are visible than actual soil, then it is time to repot.

Moreover, if no new growth has been seen for weeks during the regular growing season and watering is more frequent than normal, the pothos likely need to be repotted in a bigger pot.

FERTILIZING

Pothos are low feeders, and if using fresh potting soil mix that already contains nutrients, fertilizing once or twice a year more than suffices, especially for smaller pothos plants.

Adding earthworm castings to the soil mix, or to the topsoil if not repotting, will act as low dose and slow-release nutrients, which is all the pothos needs.

Be careful when using synthetic fertilizers, whether granular or liquid, to feed pothos as their higher NPK ratio (Nitrogen - Phosphorus - Potassium) can lead to burning of its roots and foliage.

Most house plants only need a fertilizer with a 3-1-2 NPK ratio. Particularly for pothos, fertilize only during the growing season.

ROOT ROT

The only way to get pothos to grow lush leaves and long vines is to first give it a strong and healthy foundation, which starts with taking good care of its roots, not just the foliage.

That is accomplished by not overwatering, having a well-draining soil, and enough light to help it not retain extra moisture for too long. But if and when root rot is suspected or discovered, it does not automatically mean the pothos can no longer be saved. The earlier it is caught, the higher the chances of saving the pothos plant.

The biggest sign of root rot is the nonstop yellowing of leaves. It often starts with the leaf on the base or closest to the roots, and the yellowing makes its way to the other leaves in the vine.

For pothos with root rot, the first thing to do is to not keep watering the plant. As mentioned, root rot in pothos is almost always due to overwatering. Sometimes the rotting is so bad that the stem or vine can easily be pulled off even without taking the plant out of the pot and removing the soil.

To determine if the pothos is suffering root rot, the best way is to remove the plant from the pot and as much of the soil as possible to thoroughly inspect the roots.

Rotting roots will be brown, mushy, soggy and will easily fall off. Remove all the rotted parts of the roots and trim them off if necessary.

Next, wash the remaining roots, if there are any left, with a mild dishwashing soap or castile soap. As an extra step, spray the roots with ahydrogen peroxide solution, which is one part hydrogen peroxide mixed with two parts water.

Afterwards, propagate or repot the pothos. If caught early and there are plenty of viable roots left in the pothos, repotting with fresh potting soil is fine.

However, if there are not many roots left or at all, propagating the remainder of the pothos is the best recourse until the plant regrows enough roots to be repotted in soil again.

But as mentioned, repotting should be an infrequent necessity for pothos, so when troubleshooting pothos if it is showing signs of malady, repotting should be a last resort and final remedy.

Unnecessary and frequent repotting will only cause disturbance and shock to pothos, which will then only contribute to its failure, not success.

If the thorough yet easy to follow steps discussed in this chapter on how to give water, light, and soil for pothos are taken, and avoid common bad practices in pothos plant care, pothos can be very forgiving with new plant parent mistakes, and with patience and discipline, will bounce back.

The key takeaways are:

1.) give your pothos access to decent amount of light, but low light doesn't mean no light;

2.) let your soil completely dry and understand leaves signs before watering; and

3.) only repot when necessary and as a last resort when troubleshooting your pothos.

POTHOS PROPAGATION

Whether trying to make pothos grow bigger and bushier, or trying to save what is left from an ailing pothos plant, propagation is the way to create more of a pothos plant.

For most varieties, pothos plants are quite easy to propagate. In fact, for a non-flowering plant, the main reason they are one of the most common houseplants and are considered invasive in the wild, are because pothos propagate easily.

However, plant parents sometimes get frustrated when they are not always successful with their propagation. Their cuttings yellow and rot before they can form roots; or when they have formed roots, they die when they are transferred into soil.

Not all varieties will propagate at the same rate either. Epipremnum and Philodendron pothos have faster rates of growing roots and successfully propagating compared to Scindapsus pothos, which typically are much slower growers and their cuttings do not always successfully propagate.

To have better success in propagating any pothos, it is best to start from a healthy plant. Proper pothos care can ensure the cuttings made from pothos plants will have higher rates of successful propagation.

However, if propagating pothos to save whatever is left of an ailing plant, then the same techniques in propagation also apply, but with varying success rates depending on the health and condition, as well as the number of cuttings.

PRUNING YOUR POTHOS

Aside from properly taking care of pothos, pruning pothos regularly will help to make them grow bushier leaves and trail long healthy vines. One of the reasons pothos start to grow bald when it has been trailing is because the pothos is spending most of its energy growing and providing nutrients to the vines instead of shooting growth from the top.

The weight of the vines also tugs the plant down, and sometimes even uproots the pothos. To prevent that, pin the pothos vines to the base using bobby pins. At the same time, it will put nodes in contact with soil, which can lead to new root growth and shoot out new growth from the top.

When the vines in your pothos start to look leggy– meaning the internodes or the distance between leaves are getting longer, the new growth is smaller, and sometimes non-existent, and the stem has nodes but not leaves, which are also called runners, then it is time to prune.

HOW TO MAKE POTHOS CUTTINGS

There are many ways to propagate houseplants, but for pothos, the most common way is also the best way to propagate, which is via leaf or tip cuttings.

In order to have the least amount of leaf lost and not waste more pothos vines when making cuttings, look for vines where leaves have already fallen off and cut near that leafless node.

If cutting a long vine to propagate, further divide them into smaller cuttings, and it is best to make sure each cutting has one more node than leaves. Meaning, if it has two leaves, then it should have three nodes; if it has three leaves, then it should have four nodes. This might mean having to cut offleaves in order to expose a node in the pothos cutting.

When deciding on which vines to propagate from, cut at least half inch away from both sides of the node at a forty-five-degree angle. Cutting too close or too far from the node can influence how well the cuttings will propagate. Too much stem will likely rot first, too little stem from the node will give little to no space for the cutting to grow new roots and new leaves.

It is very much possible to have single leaf cuttings (one leaf with one node) and still successfully propagate. However, it presents higher risk because single leaf cuttings often can yellow and die before they will grow roots, and there will be no additional grow points and leaves to keep the cutting viable for continued propagation.

One possible explanation to this is either the single leaf is photosynthesizing but there are no roots to process all that energy, or the growing roots are requiring too much energy, but the single leaf cannot photosynthesize fast enough, so the single leaf cutting ends up cannibalizing itself.

Same concept applies if trying to propagate a single long vine (more than three or leaves in a vine). Every time we make a cutting, we are disturbing the pothos' metabolic process. It will then make a conflicting choice between using the little energy it has to grow roots or support the vines. At some point it will fail to continue to try to do both before it can grow enough roots or push out new leaves, and therefore fail to root before it rots.

PROPAGATING POTHOS IN WATER

Pothos are commonly propagated in water, which subjectively is not always the best medium to propagate in, but certainly can do the job. This method is the easiest and most accessible and does not require a lot of experience and attention during the propagation process.

To successfully propagate pothos in water, follow these steps:

- Use a dark color container instead of a clear one, like an amber bottle or a ceramic container, wherein light cannot easily pass through. Roots are encouraged to grow in the dark more than in the light.

- Do not put propagations by the windowsill when it is cold. Pothos need temperatures above 68 degrees Fahrenheit or 20 degrees Celsius in order tostart growing roots. Using a heat mat during cold weather season will help speed up root propagation.

- Change the water regularly instead of topping it off when the water level goes down. Pothos cuttings will use up the oxygen in the water as they try to grow new roots, and they will have a hard time to do so if the oxygen in wateris depleted.

- Wait until cuttings develop secondary roots before transferring into soil, but do not keep propagations in water too long because the roots they will develop will be more suited for processing oxygen in water but not in soil.

PROPAGATING IN INERT MEDIUMS

For more experienced plant parents, success is often found in propagating pothos (and most houseplants) in inert mediums, such as: cococoir, sphagnum moss, perlite, LECA, etc., or directly in soil.

When pothos propagates in water, it develops a root structure that enables it to break down oxygen in water and from the air above the water, which is a completely different root structure it needs to break down oxygen and nutrients in soil.

Therefore, when pothos cuttings in water are transplanted into soil, sometimes the cuttings experience severe shock transplant and then die when repotted in soil.

Propagating in inert mediums allow the pothos to develop a root structure it needs to be able to survive and thrive in soil, and thus making the transition to soil less stressful than from water.

Inert medium provides a similar environment as soil in order to grow, but unlike soil, they are sterile and do not contain any nutrients or microorganisms that plant cuttings do not know how or need to utilize yet.

When propagating in inert mediums, here are a few things to keep in mind:

- If using coco coir, rehydrate it with boiling water to kill any fungus gnat eggs it might have. Sphagnum moss can be sterilized the same way;

- Check if the coco coir does not have high sodium content;

- After rehydrating coco coir or sphagnum moss, and squeeze out as much as water as possible before wrapping the cuttings with the moss or inserting them in coco coir;

- Do not let the sphagnum moss or coco coir dry out but do not let it be overly moist either because it will cost cuttings to rot; and

- If using perlite, vermiculite, LECA or other similar medium, use a container without drainage holes or have a cache pot, and fill it with water up to the level wherein it reaches only the bottom third of the inert medium. Water will reach the cuttings through capillary action.

If mass propagating pothos but do have inert mediums on hand, start with water propagation. Once the cuttings grow secondary roots, transfer it first to an inert medium, let them grow more roots, and then finally transplant into soil.

Secondary roots are the roots that form from the main root. Often plant parents tend to transplant cuttings when they see a couple of inches of the main root grow, but the cuttings are still immature to be able to handle the transplant shock into soil.

On the opposite end, when pothos propagations are left in water way too long, they would have formed a full root structure already fully adapted to break down oxygen to survive in water but not in soil.

Direct soil propagation is another method which most plant growers use, but plant enthusiasts should use this method with caution. This method requires giving the cuttings the most ideal condition with light, temperature, soil moisture level and humidity level to be able to successfully propagate with the least amount of cutting loss. Using propagation boxes or indoor greenhouses is recommended.

A mistake often made with pothos propagations is to prematurely combine them with the mother plant after they have grown some roots. What then often happens is either the mother plant gets root rot, because it is getting watered more often for the sake of the new propagations; or the new propagation dies because it fails to adapt to the drier soil environment and process nutrients the same way the mother plant already does.

Instead, pothos propagations are better off if potted separately and let them establish themselves as their own plant before combining with the mother plant.

With this method, the worst-case scenario is the newly established plant becomes the new mother plant when the original one failed to bounce back from its ailment. The best-case scenario is that the new pothos plant can be combined with the mother plant to give a fuller bushier appearance.

Key takeaways when propagating pothos:

1. When making cuttings, have one more node than number of leaves, and no more than three leaves with four nodes, for a higher success rate;

2. When water propagating, place cuttings in darker containers, change water often and keep it in warmer temperatures to encourage faster root growth;

3. When using inert mediums (coco coir, sphagnum moss) to propagate, keep them moist but not oversaturated to avoid rotting; and

4. Allow propagations to grow secondary roots before transplanting in soil.

BONUS POTHOS PROPAGATION HACK

Sometimes when making cuttings, there are vines with nodes but without any leaves. Instead of throwing them away, stick those nodes into the soil of the mother plant (yes, the mother plant!) and care for pothos normally. Eventually, those nodes will start to shoot out new leaves.

Sticking in nodes into the soil will not do any harm to the mother plant, and the worst thing that can happen is the nodes stuck in the soil will not grow new leaves or vines.

BONUS CHAPTER EXCERPTS FROM HOUSE PLANTS BACK TO BASICS

HOW TO FLUSH HOUSE PLANTS

Flushing house plants is a process of getting rid of fertilizer salt and hard water mineral buildup in the plant's soil. It is also the process used to get rid of excess nutrients from over fertilization.

While this process is more often done by those who grow tomatoes and cannabis, flushing is also beneficial for house plants, especially right before fertilizing them again at the start of the growing season. It is recommended to flush house plants every six months, and before fertilizing (or after, if over-fertilized).

To flush house plants, three times the amount of water is needed compared to when normally watering plants. The same type of water used to water house plants regularly can be used to flush plants. It does not have to be a special type of water.

However, if desired to go the extra mile, use distilled water, filtered water, or pH6 water. There are also solutions that can be added to the water specifically for flushing plants.

But before flushing, remove the top inch or so of the soil on the plant, where a lot of the buildup can be seen. Do this carefully and without disturbing the roots.

If the plant is in a terracotta pot, buildup can also be seen on the sides of the pot. It is the white stuff that accumulates on the side of the pot, which can be easily wiped or washed off.

After that, pour water slowly and in batches on top of the soil and let it drain out fully. Do not let the plant sit in the water, for it will only sip back the water in, which defeats the purpose of flushing your plant. Let the waterflow through and drain out completely at the bottom as water is being poured from the top.

After flushing and draining the plant of excess water as much as possible, the soil will still be oversaturated. To avoid root rot, give the plant as much air circulation, warmer temperatures, and light to help it evaporate the excess moisture as fast as possible. Lastly, top dress the house plant with a fresh potting soil mix and/or soil nutrients of choice.

YELLOWING LEAVES IN HOUSE PLANTS

One of the most common issues with house plants is yellowing leaves. Trying to figure out what is the cause and how to remedy them can be confusing and stressful, especially for new plant parents.

While plant parents wish there is one answer and one solution as to why house plants experience yellowing leaves, it does not have to be a death sentence for house plants, and it could be a great learning experience for plant parents to get to know their houseplants a little bit more.

Causes for yellowing leaves differ from each variety of house plants, the environment they are in, and how we take care of them.

Here are seven reasons to help determine why house plants are having yellow leaves and how to remedy them:

1. Natural Ending of Life Cycle

Often, a yellow leaf is the leaf reaching the end of its life cycle. It does not mean the plant is experiencing any issues.

This often happens among the oldest leaves in the plant, which are usually found at the base, and among leaves that have white variegation. The whiter variegation a leaf has, the shorter its lifespan due to its inability to photosynthesize.

REMEDY: When the yellowing happens to only one or two mature leaves at a time, there is nothing to worry about. Simply remove the yellowing leaf so that the plant does not spend any more energy trying to keep it alive and use it for the younger leaves of the plant.

2. Watering Issues

This is the most common reason for yellowing leaves: underwatering, overwatering, and inconsistent watering.

Underwatering – while many plants thrive on neglect and are forgiving when forgotten to water them, some plants cannot afford to get too dry before watering or be too dry for too long. As an act of self-preservation, leaves will start to yellow as it diverts nutrients and energy to other parts of the plant.

Overwatering – this is a common mistake or habit committed by new plant parents, overwatering their houseplants. Overwatering can mean twothings: watering too often and watering the plant with more water than it needs, but the soil does not dry up fast enough. Yellowing leaves then can happen as a sign of root rot.

Inconsistent watering – some plants, like the fiddle leaf fig, rubber trees, and even some pothos such as the Cebu Blue pothos, thrive on consistency.Their soil cannot get too dry for an extended period, but they do not like wet feet either. These plants do not do well with extremes and prefer being watered consistently.

REMEDY: Investing in a moisture meter might be beneficial for new plants parents to help them determine if their plants need watering. Download apps that help with tracking plants' watering schedule, especially with a large plant collection. Bottom watering plants is best to ensure plants are getting the right amount of water each time.

3. Pest Pressures or Viral/Bacterial Infection

Sometimes yellowing leaves happen due to pest pressures, and/or viral or bacterial infection. It can be hard to determine this during the early stages because the pests are not as visible to the naked eye yet and no signs of root rot or other visible damage to the plant.

However, when yellowing of leaves continues to be persistent and spreads, and the plant shows other signs of distress (such as leaf curling, wilting, holes in leaves, etc.), the likely culprit is pest or viral/bacterial infection.

> **REMEDY:** Inspect the plant more than once to determine if it is pest pressures, especially under the leaves and close to the base of the petiole, where pests like mealy bugs and scales like to be. For most pest pressures, thoroughly washing the leaves and spraying them with houseplant pest repellent (commercial or homemade) often does the trick, though for some it takes longer and requires multiple applications. Remove leaves that are severely infected.
>
> However, if the root of the problem is a possible viral or bacterial infection, plants often have little or no chance of bouncing back. Best way to save the plant is to cut off parts of the plants that are still healthy and propagate them into a new plant.

4. Soil Imbalance

Lack of Nutrients - Plants, when given the right amount of water and light, have pretty much everything they need to survive. However, plants that are in the same soil and planter for quite some time, a year or more, likely need its soil nutrients replenished.

Sometimes this is manifested when an old leaf dies out as a new leaf comes in, but not always. Fertilizing the plants can help with replenishing the soil nutrients during the growing season.

However, like with repotting, fertilizing should not be the first recourse in troubleshooting house plants, and it is best to first identify accurately the issue with the house plant before applying any fertilizer as remedy.

Over Fertilizing – Houseplants do not need high levels of NPK nutrients when fertilized. A lot of plants also do not need to be fertilized during the non-growing season; and depending on the fertilizer used, house plants do not need to be fertilized every month, let alone every week, during the growing season.

Fertilizing plants too much and too often can also lead to yellowing leaves and leaf burns. If plants are overfertilized, flushing plants can help leech excess nutrients, and then using a fertilizer that is milder and less often.

Imbalanced Soil pH – this can differ from plant to plant, some prefer a slightly acidic soil while others prefer a more neutral pH level. In general, house plants prefer a pH level between pH 5.5 to pH 6.5, which is slightly acidic. Without the right soil pH, plants cannot properly process oxygen and nutrients in soil.

REMEDY: Use a soil testing kit or digital tool to test the pH level of the soil, and to do a nutrient analysis of the nitrogen, phosphorus and potassium content in the soil. However, plant beginners might find this too daunting or unnecessary. Flushing soil and reintroducing the right amount of nutrients back into the soil, or repotting the plants with a fresh soil mix or into a new medium, is a quicker and easier solution to nutrient imbalance and soil pH issues.

5. Adjusting to New Medium

When plants are recently repotted or transferred into a new medium, like from soil to LECA or from water to soil, or simply transplanted into a larger pot, plants can experience shock, and yellowing leaves is how they manifest it.

The key here is patience and to give plant time to adjust to its new home. However, if yellowing continues to persist for a long time, the new medium it is in might not be ideal for the plant.

REMEDY: Give plants at least two weeks to adjust to their new medium and try to keep its environment as consistent as possible (do not change the amount light it receives and change up its watering schedule drastically at the same time). Yellowing normally slows down as it recovers and stops when fully adjusted to its new home.

However, if the plant's condition continues to deteriorate, then the new medium is likely not suitable for your plant. At the same time, leaf loss, and possibly root rot, are possible when switching into different media.

6. Humidity

When plants are receiving the right amount of water and light, and it is in a compatible medium, but the plant is still forming yellow leaves, humidity, or lack thereof, is likely the issue. This is often coupled with pest pressures. Plants like a humidity level between 40 and 60 percent, and the average humidity level in most households is 30 percent and below, and only 10 percent during the winter season.

REMEDY: Using a humidifier, improving air circulation, opening your windows whenever possible, or taking your plants outside when weather is sunny and between 68- and 75-degrees Fahrenheit, or between 20 and 23 degrees Celsius, can help with increasing humidity for your houseplants.

7. Location, Location, Location

Sometimes, when we think we have given all the plant needs, it is still producing yellow leaves simply because it does not like where it is positioned.

REMEDY: Move it to different spots until it finds its happy place. Often, plants will tell us where it wants to be rather than letting us put them where we want them to go. However, some plants also act up because we keep moving them around, such as the fiddle leaf fig, whichnotoriously do not like getting constantly moved. It is then best to keep them in the space they are in.

2022 PLANTIFUL PLANNER NOW AVIALABLE!

2022 Plantiful Planner is a 12 month planner with monthly and weekly spreads, food journal to plan or track your meals and water intake, habit trackers, mood trackers, as well as intentions for 2022, and bucket lists for each season.

What makes this planner unique is it is geared for plant parents, and it includes houseplant guides, plant inventory, wishlist plants spread, seasonal plant care checklists, and houseplant watering and plant care trackers for each month.

Each spread is in a bullet journal style template, and there are four additional bland dotted pages to create your own spreads, and six lined pages for your notes in each month.

Available for purchase on Amazon: https://amzn.to/3pMfhIb

REFERENCES

Boyce, P.C., and J. Bogner. “Scindapsus lucens (Araceae: Monsteroideae), a new species related to Scindapsus pictus.” *Kew Bulletin*,vol. 49, no. 4, 1994, pp. 789-791. *Aroid.org*, https://www.aroid.org/gallery/boyce/Scindapsus%20 lucens%20-%20Bogner%20%26%20Boyce%201994.pdf. Accessed 1 November 2020.

Boyce, Peter. “A Review of Epipremnum (Araceae) in Cultivation.” *Aroideana*, no. 27, 2004, p. 199_205. *www.aroid.org*, https://www.aroid.org/gallery/ boyce/A%20Review%20of%20Epipremnum%20%28Araceae %29%20in%20cultivation%20-%20%5BAroideana%2027 %2C%20199_205%5D%20-%20Boyce%202004.pdf. Accessed 12 June 2020.

Douglass, Lara. “How Long Can Pothos Ivy Live?” *SFGate*, 2020, https://homeguides.sfgate.com/long-can-pothos-ivy-live-89690.html. Accessed 15 August 2020.

Florida Foundation Seed Producers, Inc. “Green Genie™ ‘UFM10.’” *http://www.ffsp.net/*, 2013, http://www.ffsp.net/varieties/pothos/green-genie-ufm10/. Accessed 30 September 2020.

Gabriella Plants. “Identifying Philodendron Hederaceum Sports.” *Gabriella Plants*, 2020, https://www.gabriellaplants.com/pages/philodendron-hederaceum- identifying-sports. Accessed 30 August 2020.

Glasshouse Works. "Philodendron scandens variegatum." *Glasshouse Works*, 2020, http://www.glasshouseworks.com/philodendron-scandens-variegatum. Accessed 10 September 2020.

Happy Houseplants. *Facebook.com*, 20 June 2019, https://www.facebook.com/200202397253140/posts/epipremnum-aureum-is-sometimes-called-commonly-the-javelin-shangri-la-or-sleepin/408058719800839/. Accessed 15 September 2020.

Henny, Richard J., et al. "Epipremnum aureum 'Green Genie.'" *HortScience*, vol. 44, no. 6, 2009, pp. 1783-1784. https://doi.org/10.21273/HORTSCI.44.6.1783

House Plant Hobbyist. "Epipremnum Pinnatum 'Skeleton Key' Care." *House Plant Hobbyist*, 3 March 2020, https://www.house-plant- hobbyist.com /blog/2020/2/20/epipremnum-pinnatum-skeleton-key-care.Accessed 20 September 2020.

Hung, Chiu-Yueh, et al. "Gibberellin deficiency is responsible for shy-flowering nature of Epipremnum aureum." *Scientific Reports. nature.com*, https://www.nature.com/articles/srep28598.pdf.

Ianotti, Marie. "Pothos Plant Profile." *The Spruce*, 20 May 2020, https://www.thespruce.com/pothos-an-easy-to-grow-houseplant-1403154. Accessed 15 August 2020.

International Aroid Society, Inc. "Scindapsus Pictus 'Platinum.'" *International Aroid Society, Inc. Cultivar Wiki*, 26 August 2016, http://www.aroid.org/cvwiki/index.php/Scindapsus_pictus_%E2%80%98Pl atinum%E2%80%99. Accessed 15 September 2020.

Leafy Place. "Types of Pothos Plants (Epipremnum Aureum) &Identification (Pictures & Names)." *Leafyplace.com*, 2020, https://leafyplace.com/types-of-pothos-plants/. Accessed 1 October 2020.

Monstera Mike. "Have you heard of this plant? The New Global Green Pothos." *youtube.com*, 21 May 2020, https://www.youtube.com/watch?v=o4m9UqdI3-E. Accessed 15 September 2020.

New Life Tropicals. "Epipremnum aureum 'Shangri Ooh La La.'" *New Life Tropicals*, 2017, https://www.newlifetropicals.com/product/541. Accessed16 October 2020.

North Carolina State Extension. "Epipremnum Aureum." *North Carolina Extension Gardener Plant Toolbox*, 2020, https://plants.ces.ncsu.edu /plants/epipremnum-aureum/. Accessed 31 08 2020.

The Plant List. "Species in Scindapsus." *The Plant List*, 2013, http://www.theplantlist.org/1.1/browse/A/Araceae/Scindapsus/. Accessed 1 November 2020.

Rewild DC. "Scindapsus Green Satin." *Rewild DC*, 2020, https://rewilddc.com/products/scindapsus-green-satin. Accessed 20 October 2020.

Stuart Change. "Philippine Medicinal Plants." *Tibatib*, 2017, http://www.stuartxchange.org/Tabatib. Accessed November 2020.

ACKNOWLEDGEMENTS

The Ultimate Guide to Pothos Plants would not have been possible without the support of subscribers and followers of *My Wasteless Life* on YouTube and Instagram, where I take my fellow plant lovers along my plant journey, and share with them beginner tips and tricks on house plants and sustainable lifestyle.

I would like to especially thank the following plant enthusiasts, experts, sellers and growers who gave me permission to use the pictures of their pothos plants in this book: my subscribers and plant friends Jas Villa, Raciel Flores, and Michael; plant sellers and plant Instagrammers @much.greens, @the.plantnurse, @earthplants.id, @rav_house, @1000tropicalaroid, @peaceloveandhappiness.club and @pothosloco; Shane Maloy from Gabriella Plants; and Sarah from Glasshouse Works.

Thank you so much to viewers, subscribers, plant friends, the online plant community, and my family for supporting my plant journey and allowing me to share with you my love of pothos and house plants. I see you, I appreciate you, and have a plantiful day!

ABOUT THE AUTHOR

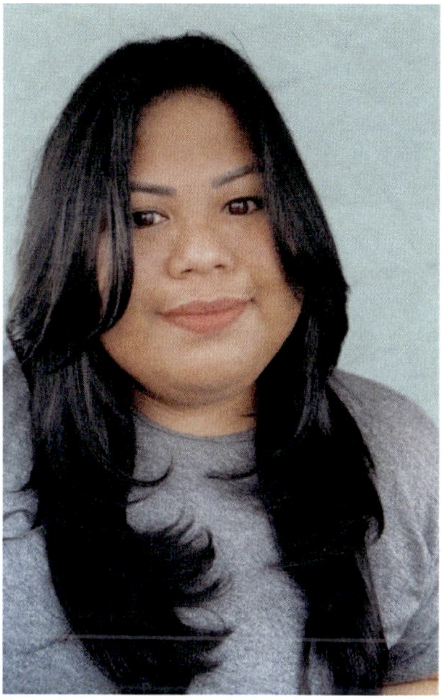

Marianne Baesa is a house plant enthusiast and a sustainable lifestyle advocate, and the content creator behind *My Wasteless Life*, where she documents her plant and sustainable lifestyle journey on YouTube, Tiktok and Instagram (@mywastelesslife). She also coaches plant beginners on how to take care of their house plants and is most known for her pothos collection.

She currently resides in Maryland with her family and pet dog, Theodore Bentley.